# Hunter's Money Jar

Written by
Charlotte Guillain

Illustrated by
Duncan Beedie

**PEARSON**

ISBN-13: 978-0-328-83275-0
ISBN-10: 0-328-83275-8

11  20

Scratch lived with her friends in Hunter's money jar.

Scratch lived with some other coins. Ridge and Hex were her best friends. Together, they looked after all the little shiny coins.

There were some bills in the jar too.

Rip's in charge of the jar. He's OK, but he can be a bit bossy sometimes. A lot of the bills are like that!

Hunter had been saving up to buy a skateboard for a long time. He counted his coins and bills every day. But there wasn't enough money in his jar yet.

7

It was Hunter's birthday, and he was really excited. He found some money in one of his cards!

A new bill! Maybe Hunter will have enough of us for a skateboard now. I hope he counts us soon. I want to find out!

But Hunter didn't
count the bills and
coins. He wanted to
take them somewhere.

Hunter knew exactly what he was looking for. He walked through aisles of toys until he found it. The skateboard! He hoped he had enough money to buy it.

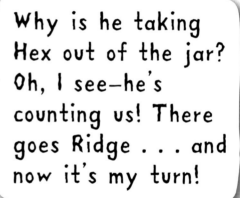

Hunter counted up his coins and bills. It wasn't enough! He was so disappointed.

Why is he taking Hex out of the jar? Oh, I see—he's counting us! There goes Ridge . . . and now it's my turn!

The shop owner tried to sell
Hunter a cheaper skateboard
instead. Hunter wasn't sure
what to do.

Don't do it, Hunter! Keep saving up for the really good skateboard. Don't waste us on that one. It's not as good!

Hunter looked at the cheaper skateboard. He thought carefully. Then he decided to wait. He would keep saving until he had enough money for the skateboard he really wanted.

Hunter decided to hold a yard sale
to sell the toys he had outgrown.

The yard sale was going well. More coins were dropped into the jar.

Hi, guys! Welcome to Hunter's money jar. Scoot over, everyone! Look—Hunter's selling his old plane now. Here comes a new bill!

Hunter counted the money again. It still wasn't enough! So he offered to help his mom and dad with chores. They seemed pleased about that!

Hunter's mom and dad gave him some new coins.

Phew, it's getting a bit crowded in here now!

It was time for Hunter to count again. Would he have enough money? He put the bills into neat piles. He stacked the coins carefully . . .

Hunter was so happy! He had saved up for so long. He was going to have lots of fun with his new skateboard.

And me? Well, the cash register is my new home. I live here with all my friends! I wonder what my next adventure will be . . .